The Medieval World

Medieval Projects You Can Do!

Marsha Groves

Crabtree Publishing Company

www.crabtreebooks.co

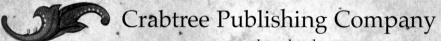

Crabtree Publishing Company

www.crabtreebooks.com

Coordinating editor: Ellen Rodger

Series and project editor: Carrie Gleason

Designer and production coordinator: Rosie Gowsell

Production assistant: Samara Parent

Scanning technician: Arlene Arch-Wilson

Art director: Rob MacGregor

Crafts and photography: Rosie Gowsell, Allison Napier

Project development, editing, photo editing, and layout:
First Folio Resource Group, Inc.: Tom Dart, Sarah Gleadow, Debbie Smith

Photo research: Maria DeCambra

Photographs: Alinari/Art Resource, NY: p. 8; Art Archive/San Alberto di Butrio Abbey Ponte Nizza/Dagli Orti: p. 28 (bottom); British Library/Add. 27697 f.197: p. 20; British Library/Cotton Claudius D. II f.33: p. 14; British Library/HIP/The Image Works: p. 10 (top), p. 22 (top), p. 24; British Library/Royal 14.E.IV f.210: p. 16; Giraudon/Art Resource, NY: p. 12 (top); Glasgow University Library/Bridgeman Art Library: p. 31; Erich Lessing/Art Resource, NY: p. 18 (top); Réunion des Musées Nationaux/Art Resource, NY: title page; Scala/Art Resource, NY: cover, p. 4; Victoria & Albert Museum, London/Art Resource, NY: p. 6 (top); Walters Art Museum, Baltimore/Bridgeman Art Library: p. 26 (top)

Illustrations: Katherine Kantor: flags, title page (border), copyright page (bottom); Margaret Amy Salter: borders, gold boxes, title page (illuminated letter), copyright page (top), contents page (background), p. 4 (pyramid)

Cover: Medieval women, including noblewomen, learned weaving, embroidery, and other textile crafts.

Title page: In the Great Hall, the most important room in the noble's home, the walls were covered with magnificent tapestries of battle scenes, the table was set with gold platters, and guests were welcomed to feasts.

Crabtree Publishing Company

www.crabtreebooks.com   1-800-387-7650

Cataloging-in-Publication Data

Groves, Marsha.
    Medieval projects you can do! / written by Marsha Groves.
       p. cm. -- (The medieval world series)
    Includes index.
    ISBN-13: 978-0-7787-1361-6 (RLB)
    ISBN-10: 0-7787-1361-X (RLB)
    ISBN-13: 978-0-7787-1393-7 (pbk)
    ISBN-10: 0-7787-1393-8 (pbk)
  1. Middle Ages--History. 2. Civilization, Medieval. 3. Europe--Social life and customs. I. Title. II. Medieval worlds series
    D117.G76 2005
    940.1--dc22

                                    2005014780
                                    LC

**Published in
the United States**
PMB 16A
350 Fifth Ave.
Suite 3308
New York, NY
10118

**Published
in Canada**
616 Welland Ave.
St. Catharines
Ontario, Canada
L2M 5V6

**Published in the
United Kingdom**
73 Lime Walk
Headington
Oxford
OX3 7AD
United Kingdom

**Published
in Australia**
386 Mt. Alexander Rd.
Ascot Vale (Melbourne)
VIC 3032

Table of Contents

The Middle Ages

The Middle Ages, or medieval period, lasted from about 500 A.D. to 1500 A.D. in western Europe. During this time, lords, including kings and important nobles, controlled large territories and had great power. They rewarded their supporters, who were less important nobles and knights, with smaller landholdings called manors.

Most people in the Middle Ages were peasants. Peasants lived on manors and in other small settlements in the countryside. They farmed the land using mainly hand-held tools, horses, and oxen. Other people, including many types of craftspeople and tradespeople, lived in towns and cities.

Supplies for Living

Without factories or complex machinery, medieval people made many of the things they needed by hand. They spun their own thread and yarn to make cloth, cooked and **preserved** their own food, and carved toys and tools from wood. Items that people did not make themselves, they bought or **bartered** for, with craftspeople and tradespeople.

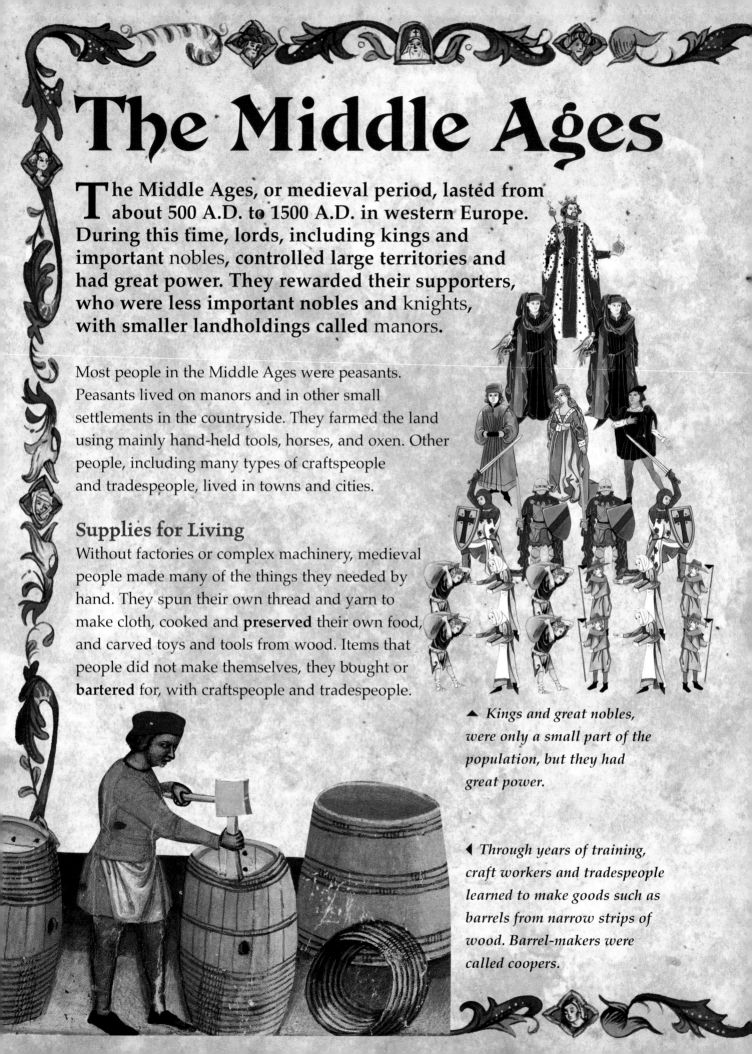

▲ *Kings and great nobles, were only a small part of the population, but they had great power.*

◀ *Through years of training, craft workers and tradespeople learned to make goods such as barrels from narrow strips of wood. Barrel-makers were called coopers.*

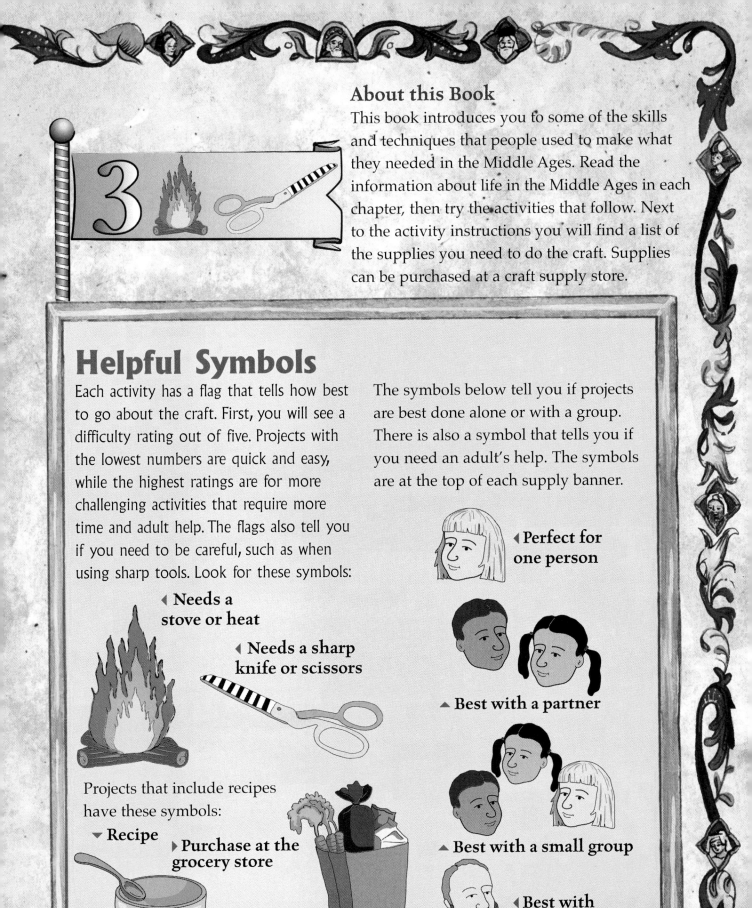

About this Book

This book introduces you to some of the skills and techniques that people used to make what they needed in the Middle Ages. Read the information about life in the Middle Ages in each chapter, then try the activities that follow. Next to the activity instructions you will find a list of the supplies you need to do the craft. Supplies can be purchased at a craft supply store.

Helpful Symbols

Each activity has a flag that tells how best to go about the craft. First, you will see a difficulty rating out of five. Projects with the lowest numbers are quick and easy, while the highest ratings are for more challenging activities that require more time and adult help. The flags also tell you if you need to be careful, such as when using sharp tools. Look for these symbols:

The symbols below tell you if projects are best done alone or with a group. There is also a symbol that tells you if you need an adult's help. The symbols are at the top of each supply banner.

◀ **Perfect for one person**

◀ **Needs a stove or heat**

◀ **Needs a sharp knife or scissors**

▲ **Best with a partner**

Projects that include recipes have these symbols:

▼ **Recipe**

▶ **Purchase at the grocery store**

▲ **Best with a small group**

◀ **Best with an adult**

Medieval Dress

Most clothing in the Middle Ages was made of sheep's wool. The wool was sometimes scratchy and rough and sometimes smooth and soft, depending on the fineness of its weave.

Cloth was woven on a rectangular wooden frame called a loom. Strong threads, called the warp, were fastened lengthwise along the loom. The weaver wrapped another thread, the weft, on a holder called a shuttle. Using the shuttle, the weaver passed the weft up and down between the warp threads. When the other side of the loom was reached, the weaver tightened the weave by pushing the new row snugly against the previous one. Then, the weft was woven back to the other side. The more rows that were woven, the longer the piece of cloth.

◄ *Men in the Middle Ages wore knee-length, long-sleeved overshirts, called tunics, over undershirts and close-fitting leggings. Women wore ankle-length tunics over chemises, which were calf-length undershirts.*

▶ *Use the activity on the next page to weave your own belt, headband, wristband, or small mat on a cardboard loom.*

Learn to Weave

1. Cut the top flaps off the box.

2. Draw lines 1/4 inch (5 mm) deep and 1/4 inch (5 mm) apart on the top of the box. Cut a slot at each line.

3. Tape one end of the warp thread below the first slot. Wrap the warp all the way around the box, slipping it into opposite slots. Use tape to secure the string.

Supplies

- Large, sturdy cardboard box
- Ruler
- Pencil
- Scissors
- Strong white cotton string (warp thread)
- Masking tape
- Thin dowel
- Cardboard cut into butterfly shapes
- Different colored yarns

weft

warp

4. Slide the dowel under and over alternate warp threads.

5. Cut out and wrap yarn around butterfly-shaped pieces of cardboard. These are the shuttles.

6. Unwrap a length of yarn from a shuttle that is slightly wider than your project. Pass the yarn beneath the raised warp threads. Leave some yarn dangling at the beginning of the row.

shuttle

7. Tighten the weft by sliding the dowel toward the yarn. Then remove the dowel and reweave so the opposite warp threads are elevated. Pass the shuttle back across the warp.

8. Change shuttles to use a different color of yarn. Repeat step 7 until your weaving is complete.

9. To finish your weaving, remove the tape and cut the warp strings near the bottom of the box. Gently lift the cloth from the loom, holding the warp. Tie pieces of warp threads together to make a fringe and trim them with scissors. Tuck any loose ends of weft thread into the edge of the weaving.

dowel

3

Everyday Food

In the Middle Ages, most everyday meals were made with grains, such as wheat, barley, rye, and oats. Pulses, such as peas, beans, and lentils, were also eaten. Peasants grew these foods in fields. People also ate eggs, fish, some meat, and cooked fruits and vegetables when they were in season.

Making it Last

Some **perishable** foods were preserved, so they were available throughout the year. Fish was gutted, dried, covered with salt, and packed in barrels. Some meats and olives were soaked in a salty liquid called brine, then drained and packed in salt. Eggs were preserved in water mixed with a chemical called alum. Meat that was butchered was salted and smoked.

▶ *Every household grew herbs in small garden plots. Some herbs were dried for use later in the year.*

Make a Simple Pottage

Pottage was a one-pot meal. Some pottages were thick mixtures of grains and pulses. Fancier pottages, which were more like stews, combined meat, vegetables, spices, and breadcrumbs.

Directions

1. Combine barley, peas, lentils, water, and salt in a saucepan. Bring to a boil uncovered.

2. Boil for one minute, then lower the heat to a gentle simmer. Cover with a lid.

3. Stir every ten minutes. If the mixture seems dry, add water, a half-cup at a time. The pottage is ready after 30 or 40 minutes, when the peas and lentils are tender, .

4. For extra flavor, add finely chopped fresh herbs, greens, feta cheese, or butter to the hot pottage. Stir well.

Drying Flowers and Herbs

Dried herbs, such as mint, oregano, thyme, and rosemary, were used to flavor food and make medicines or **dyes**. Dried flowers, such as marigolds, lavender, and roses, added a pleasant scent to the home.

Directions

1. Tie together small bunches of fresh herbs or flowers for drying.

2. Hang the bunches upside down on hangers or coat hooks. Place them in a dry, airy spot, away from direct sunlight.

3. After about two weeks, crumble the dried herbs and flowers. Place them in small bowls to scent rooms.

Pottage Ingredients

- 1/2 cup (125 mL) dry pearl barley
- 1/4 cup (60 mL) dry split peas
- 1/4 cup (60 mL) dry green lentils
- 3 1/4 cups (800 mL) water
- 1/2 tsp (2 mL) salt
- A handful of fresh mint, parsley, or spinach
- Feta cheese
- Butter

Pottage Supplies

- Measuring cup
- Medium saucepan
- Wooden spoon
- Cutting board
- Sharp knife

Drying Supplies

- Assorted herbs and flowers

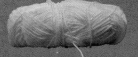

- String
- Clothes hangers or coat hooks
- Bowls

A Peasant's Home

Many peasants lived in small homes made of wooden frames. Between the frames' timbers, walls were filled in with wattle and daub.

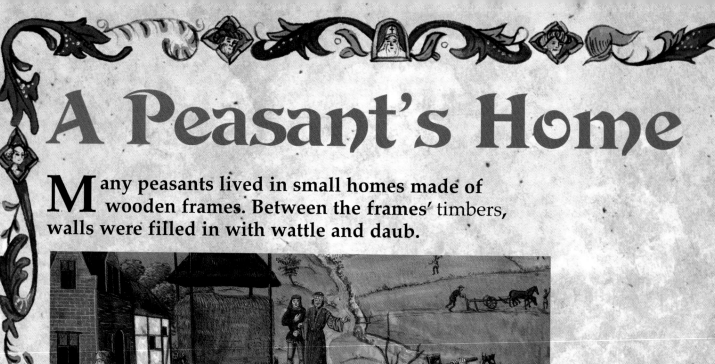

◀ *Wattle was also used to make fences and animal pens.*

Wattle was made by weaving flexible branches between wooden posts. Daub was a mixture of mud, straw, and animal dung. When the mixture was smeared, or daubed, over the wattle, it made a solid, windproof wall.

Foundation to Roof

Timber homes were often built on low foundation walls, made of **mortar** and rubble. This raised the wood off the damp ground and slowed the timbers' rotting from moisture. Long-lasting roofs were made with bundles of straw or reeds, called thatch. It took skill to build a sturdy house, and carpenters and thatchers were valued craftspeople.

▶ *To prevent damage from rain, walls were coated with whitewash, a thin paint made of a powdered mineral called lime.*

Make a Wattle-and-Daub House

1. Soak willow branches in water until they are soft and flexible. Pat them dry.

2. On a piece of cardboard, use modeling clay to make the house's foundation walls. The walls should be about 1 inch (2.5 cm) high, 1 inch (2.5 cm) thick, and form a rectangle about 8 inches (20 cm) long by 6 inches (15 cm) wide.

3. Using pruners and wearing safety goggles, cut posts from dogwood branches. The posts should be 4 inches (10 cm) tall.

4. Insert the posts in the clay walls, except at the corners. Pinch the clay firmly around each post.

5. Cut four corner posts, called crucks, from dogwood branches. The crucks should be 8 inches (20 cm) long, and a bit thinner and more flexible than the shorter posts.

crucks

6. Insert the crucks into the four corners. Bend the front crucks into an "X" shape, and tie securely with twine where they cross. Repeat with the back pair.

7. Weave the willow branches between the posts. Trim the ends. Remember to leave an open space for the door.

8. To make daub, roll and pat Plasticine into very thin sheets. Press it over the wattle.

9. To make the roof, lay a branch across the Xs of the crucks. Fold a piece of construction paper over the branch. Glue straw or raffia onto the paper in layers, starting with a row near the bottom of the roof, to make the thatch.

posts

foundation walls

In a Noble's Home

Noble families lived in castles or fortified manor houses that were usually built of stone. The most important room was the Great Hall, where members of the household gathered for meals and celebrations. Some people even slept there because there were few private bedrooms.

Castles and manor houses were heated only by fireplaces. To make rooms warmer and more welcoming, people used woven and **embroidered** cloths such as wall hangings, curtains, pillow covers, and table coverings. The largest and most elaborate wall hangings were tapestries, which look like paintings woven from silk and wool. Medieval tapestries often showed detailed scenes from history, the **Bible**, songs, and legends.

▲ *The Bayeux Tapestry is an enormous medieval wall hanging. It tells the story of how William of Normandy, known as William the Conqueror, became king of England. The Latin words on the wall hanging explain the events shown in each scene.*

▼ *Make your own medieval wallhanging.*

Once upon a time an orphaned lad called Arthur was given to a Sir Ector to raise as his own son and squire by the powerful wizard, Merlin.

The King of England had died, leaving no heir to the throne. Instead, a magical sword called Excalibur was embedded in stone. Whosoever could pull the sword from the stone would become king.

Make a Wall Hanging

Make a wall hanging that tells about something that happened in medieval Europe, or about something that happened recently in your country, community, or school.

Directions

1. Sketch simple scenes for your wall hanging on paper.

2. Make vertical lines on a long piece of cloth to divide it into the same number of sections as scenes.

3. Cut out fabric to make the pictures for your scenes. Cut several small shapes to make a large image.

4. Use a needle and thread or fabric glue to attach the fabric to the cloth background. Add details with ribbon, cord, and other trimmings.

5. With fabric markers, write a sentence to explain each scene on the wall hanging.

Supplies
- Pencils

- Paper
- Long piece of plain cloth or an old sheet
- Small pieces of fabric of different types and colors
- Scissors

- Needle and embroidery thread or fabric glue
- Beads, ribbon, cord, sequins, feathers, and other trimmings

- Fabric marker

As a young squire, Arthur accompanied Sir Ector to a tournament where knights tried to pull the sword from the stone, but none could budge it.

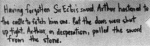

Having forgotten Sir Ector's sword, Arthur hastened to the castle to fetch him one. But the doors were shut up tight. Arthur, in desperation, pulled the sword from the stone.

And so it was that Arthur became the rightful King of England.

The Field of Honor

Knights were medieval warriors who fought to defend or gain land for their lord. They battled on horseback, with swords as their main weapons.

Knights wore armor to protect themselves in battle. By the 1100s, steel plate armor covered most of a knight's face and body. This made it difficult to know who was a friend and who was an enemy on the battlefield. To help identify themselves, knights began to add bright designs to their outer garments, or surcoats. These designs were called coats of arms. Most nobles chose symbols for their coats of arms that told something about themselves. A family with a mighty castle showed a castle in its design. A family that controlled a sea port showed a boat or a symbol that represented water.

▲ *The king of England had golden lions on his coat of arms.*

Rules of Arms

Men used coats of arms drawn in a shield shape. Women's coats of arms were drawn in a diamond shape called a lozenge. Often, coats of arms were divided into sections that showed the arms of important **ancestors** of both the husband's and wife's families. By 1250, coats of arms had become so popular that rules were put in place to make sure that no one had the same design. The system of keeping track of the designs and developing new ones is called heraldry.

Create a Coat of Arms

1. Cut a shield or lozenge shape from colored Bristol board. Choose a color from the chart. To make a metallic background, cover the Bristol board with foil or metallic paper.

Color	Meaning
Purple	Justice, royalty
Bright blue	Strength, loyalty
Red	Fierceness in battle
Emerald green	Hope, youth
Black	Sadness, misfortune
Gold	Generosity
Silver	Sincerity, peace

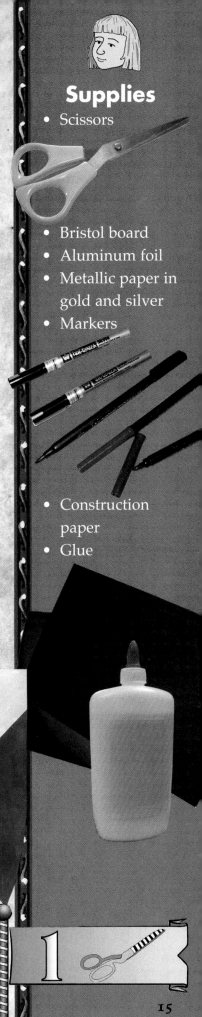

Fess
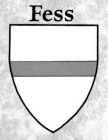

Chevron

Saltire

Bend

Beasts and Birds	Meaning
Lion	Courageous
Bear	Fierce protector
Fox	Wise, clever
Wolf	Steadfast, persistent
Griffin	Courageous
Dragon	Courageous
Eagle	Noble protector
Swan	Poetic, musical

2. Design your coat of arms. Draw wide lines to divide it into sections. Each section can be a different color. Above are four ways to divide coats of arms.

3. Make up symbols that show your name or your interests. Add some of these real and imaginary beasts and birds to your design.

4. Draw your coat of arms with markers, or cut out symbols and animals from construction paper or metallic paper. Glue your symbols onto the background.

15

Military Machines

S ome medieval battles were fought on open fields between two armies. Others were sieges, in which an army surrounded a castle or town and tried to starve out the people or force its way in and take possession.

Large machines called siege engines were used to attack castles or towns. Siege engines threw ammunition, such as boulders or metal balls. The **ammunition** smashed down the fortification's walls, crushed buildings inside, and frightened people.

Machines of Terror

The most powerful siege engine was the trebuchet. The trebuchet looked like an unequal seesaw built on a heavy wooden frame. A sling that held ammunition was attached to the long end of the trebuchet. Rocks were attached to the short end. This was called the counterweight. The long end was pulled down, and then released. This flung the long arm upward and sent the ammunition into the air toward the target.

▲ *From the tops of fortifications, defenders fired arrows on the army below.*

Build a Trebuchet

1. Lay a marker across the back of a stir stick to form a "T" shape. Use an elastic band to fasten the marker to the stick.

2. Fill a sandwich bag half-full with coins to make a counterweight. Tape the bag tightly together. Using tape, attach the counterweight to the top of the short end of the stick.

3. Tape or glue a bottle cap to the long end of the stick.

4. Stand the box upright. Fold down the top flaps and tape them against the outside of the box.

5. Use scissors to cut notches on both sides of the box, near one end of the opening. Rest the marker in the notches.

6. Place ammunition in the bottle cap. Hold the box firmly while gently pulling down on the long end of the stick. Release the stick. The trebuchet will fling the ammunition up and away.

Supplies

- Marker
- Paint stir stick

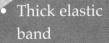

- Thick elastic band
- Plastic sandwich bag
- Coins or other weights
- Masking tape
- Bottle cap
- Glue

- Cereal box
- Scissors

- Marshmallow, Ping-Pong ball, or pompom (for ammunition)

Art in Churches

In the Middle Ages, most Europeans were Christians. Christians believe in one God and follow the teachings of Jesus Christ, who they believe is God's son.

Christians in the Middle Ages worshiped at local churches, some of which were decorated with fine art. Cathedrals, the largest and most important churches, were made bright and colorful with stained-glass windows, wall paintings, and mosaics. Mosaics are designs made of tiny glass, **ceramic**, or stone tiles laid in mortar.

▶ *Some mosaics showed decorative patterns. Others were images of kings, queens, and saints.*

Supplies

- Small foil pie plates
- Rubber gloves and smock to keep you clean
- Plaster of Paris
- Plastic mixing tub
- Paint stir stick
- Heavy paper clip or twine
- Decorative stones or glass beads

Make a Mosaic

1. Mix plaster of Paris with water until it is creamy. Pour about 1/2 inch (1 cm) of plaster into a pie plate. Make a hook for your mosaic by pressing a heavy paper clip or a loop of twine into the plaster near the top of the pie plate.

2. Press the stones or beads gently into the plaster to make a design.

3. Let the mosaic dry overnight, then slide it out of the pie plate.

3

Make a Stained-Glass Window

1. Using a grater or sharpener, shave crayons onto pieces of waxed paper. Use a different sheet of waxed paper for each color.

2. Fold the waxed paper in half. On an old towel or sheet, gently press the waxed paper with a warm iron until the crayons melt. Set the waxed paper aside to cool.

3. Draw a simple design on a piece of paper.

4. Cut out the middle of a black sheet of construction paper to make your window frame.

5. Cut out a black strip of paper to match each line in your drawing. Lay out the strips within the frame to form your drawing. Starting from the outside and working your way inward, glue the strips to each other and the frame.

6. Cut out pieces of the waxed-paper "glass". Glue the pieces onto the back of the frame and construction paper strips.

7. Hang your finished craft in a window where light can shine through it.

Making Books

In the Middle Ages, every book and document **was** written by hand by specially trained clerks and scribes. Scribes copied manuscripts **using pens made from the** quills **of goose feathers and ink mixed from** soot, **tree sap, and** oak gall.

Most books were written on parchment or vellum, which was prepared from the hides of lambs and calves. The hides were **tanned** to keep the leather flexible and to prevent it from rotting. Then, the hides were whitened with chalk and pressed smooth to make a good writing surface. Scribes marked lines and margins on each page to help keep their writing neat.

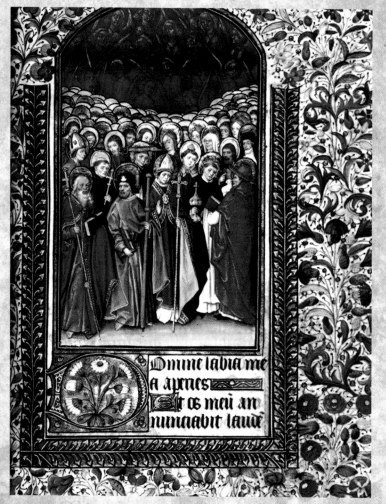

Decorative Books

Some books, such as books of prayers, had very colorful illustrations. These pictures were called illuminations because they seemed to shine with light. They were made with pressed gold, called gold leaf, paints, and colored inks. Most illuminations decorated the initial, or first, letter of a word, and usually showed scenes from the book. Scribes and artists also decorated the margins with tiny pictures of flowers, animals, and other objects from nature.

◀ *A scene from a medieval manuscript. The initial "D" is set on a background of gold leaf and is painted a vivid blue. Blue paint was made by grinding a semi-precious stone called lapis lazuli.*

An Illuminated Name Card

Use this medieval alphabet to make an illuminated name card.

a b c d e f g h i j k l m
n o p q r s t u v w x y z

Supplies

- Ruler
- Pencil

- Large, unlined index card or other white card stock
- Fine black marker or felt-tip pen

- Gold, silver, and other colored markers

Directions

1. Use a ruler and a pencil to make faint lines on an index card.

2. With a pencil, lightly sketch the initial letter of your name. This letter should be three or four times as large as the other letters.

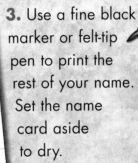

3. Use a fine black marker or felt-tip pen to print the rest of your name. Set the name card aside to dry.

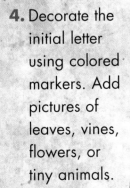

4. Decorate the initial letter using colored markers. Add pictures of leaves, vines, flowers, or tiny animals.

1

Having Fun

Medieval people enjoyed their free time and holidays by singing, dancing, and telling stories. They played games similar to tag, hide-and-seek, soccer, and field hockey. In winter, they skated on wooden or bone blades strapped to their shoes, and slid wooden discs or stones at targets on the ice.

Toys

Medieval children played with small, homemade toys, such as spinning tops and simple stuffed dolls called poppets. They also played make-believe with miniature versions of everyday items or figures, including farmyard animals, pots and pans, furniture, and knights with swords, shields, and horses.

Feasts and Holidays

Markets, fairs, and feasts were filled with many types of entertainment. There were musicians, puppet shows, jugglers, acrobats, and trained animals. On holidays, people performed religious plays that told stories from the Bible.

▲ *Musicians and acrobats were popular street performers. These men and women traveled from town to town seeking new audiences.*

▶ *Create your own puppet show.*

Make a Puppet Show

Make a puppet show about an event from the Middle Ages, or retell a legend from medieval times.

Directions

1. Make hand puppets by decorating mittens, gloves, socks, or stockings. Cut different colored fabric in the shape of eyes and mouths and glue on. Glue on yarn for hair. To make long puppets such as serpents or dragons, stuff stockings and decorate. Stick pencils into the undersides of the puppets and use them to move and wiggle the puppets along the stage.

2. Make a background for your puppet show on stiff cardboard or Bristol board.

3. Make a stage by hanging a rod between two chairs. Drape a curtain, tablecloth, or another large piece of fabric over the rod.

4. Choose a role for each person in your group. Rehearse your roles. Experiment with different ways of moving your puppets, and try different voices for your puppets' characters.

5. Perform your puppet play for friends, family, or classmates.

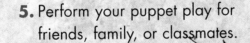

Supplies

- Mittens, gloves, socks, stockings
- Construction paper, felt, buttons, beads, yarn, fabric, pipe cleaners

- Scissors
- Scraps of cloth, crumpled paper
- Fabric glue
- Chopsticks, wooden rods, or pencils
- Cardboard
- Markers
- Long rod or pole
- Chairs
- Curtain, tablecloth, sheet, or another large piece of fabric

2

Come to the Feast!

In the Middle Ages, special meals called feasts were held to celebrate weddings, holidays, and the visits of important guests. People gathered to eat fancy food, watch entertainers, and enjoy each others' company.

Your Feast

With some adult help, you can prepare a medieval feast to celebrate an important event in your school or community, or a special time of the year. Choose from the activities on the next few pages to plan your feast. Different groups can prepare different parts of the feast.

▲ *Important guests at a feast were seated at a table covered in fine linen. Many different foods were offered at each of the meal's three courses.*

THE MENU

Menus for feasts featured fancy, decorated foods, including roasted peacocks with their feathers stuck back on, spiced meats and pies, and elaborate pastries. These dishes were made in surprising shapes, such as ships, castles, and **mythological** animals. The hosts of the feast hoped to amaze and impress their guests. Serve your guests this three-course feast.

First Course

- Small savory tarts, or mini-quiches
- Mixed green salad
- "Gilded" meatballs
- Honeyed carrots

Second Course

- Roasted chicken decorated with parsley and apple slices
- Applesauce with cinnamon

Third Course

- Small fruit tartlets
- Medieval gingerbread
- Grapes
- Dried apricots and dates
- Spiced cider

Cooking Supplies

- Large salad bowl
- Cutting board
- Sharp knife
- Wooden spoon and fork
- Measuring spoons
- Measuring cup
- Small jar with lid
- Large and small mixing bowls
- Large saucepan
- Timer
- Fork
- Skewers
- Spoon
- Baking tray
- 8 inch by 8 inch (20 cm by 20 cm) baking pan or 4 inch by 8 inch (10 cm by 20 cm) loaf pan
- Waxed paper
- Spatula

3

Food Safety

Follow these food safety rules:

1. Wash your hands thoroughly with warm, soapy water before and after handling food.
2. Wash utensils and food preparation surfaces with warm, soapy water before and after use.
3. Do not use the same cutting boards, knives, and other utensils to prepare raw and cooked foods.
4. Cook meat thoroughly.
5. Ask an adult to use the stove or oven.
6. Be aware of food allergies.

▲ *Most cooking in medieval homes took place over open fires. You will be using a hot stove and oven for your cooking. Be careful when near the heat.*

RECIPES

The following recipes make six average portions. Make multiple batches, depending on the number of guests you are serving at your feast.

Mixed Green Salad Ingredients

Leaf lettuce
1 English cucumber, diced
2 hard-boiled eggs, chopped
2 bunches watercress, stems removed
Fresh tarragon or fresh chives
Edible flowers, such as violets or
  nasturtiums (optional)
1/3 cup (80 mL) olive oil
3 tbsp (45 mL) white wine vinegar
1/2 tsp (2 mL) honey

Mixed Green Salad

Directions

1. Toss together the first six ingredients.
2. Shake the olive oil, vinegar, and honey in a small jar.
3. Pour the dressing over the salad just before serving and toss.

Gilded Meatballs

Meatball Ingredients
1 lb (.45 kg) ground
   beef, veal, or pork
1 egg yolk
1/2 tsp (2 mL) ground cloves
1/8 tsp (.5 mL) nutmeg
1/4 tsp (1 mL) ground pepper
1/4 tsp (1 mL) salt
1 tsp (5 mL) currants or chopped
   golden raisins
1 qt (1 L) water, beef or chicken
   broth

▼ *Gilding is the process of coating
something in gold. You can also "gild"
store-bought frozen meatballs.*

Meatball Directions

1. Mix together all the ingredients except the water or broth.

2. Roll the meat mixture into forms the size and shape of golf balls.

3. Boil the water in the saucepan. Place the meatballs in the pan. When the meatballs float to the surface, set a timer for six minutes.

4. After six minutes, remove the largest meatball and cut it in half to check that no pink remains. If any pink is visible, cook the meatballs for two more minutes and check again. Repeat until the meatballs are cooked through.

Gilding Ingredients
5 egg yolks
A few threads of saffron or a few
   drops of yellow food coloring
2 tbsp (30 mL) flour

Gilding Directions

1. Preheat the oven to 400°F (200°C).

2. Beat together the gilding ingredients.

3. Thread the meatballs on skewers. Place the skewers on a baking tray. Spoon or brush the gilding mixture over the meatballs and put them in the oven.

4. Bake for five minutes, then recoat the meatballs with the gilding mixture. Cook for about eight minutes or until the second coat is firm.

Honeyed Carrots

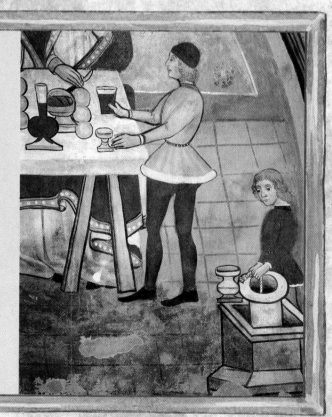

Honeyed Carrots Ingredients
4 large carrots, peeled
    and cut in rounds
Water
2 tbsp (30 mL) honey
1 tbsp (15 mL) butter

Directions

1. Place the carrots in a saucepan with about 1/2 inch (12 mm) water. Bring to a boil, lower the heat, and cover.

2. Every few minutes, shake the pan gently. Add a little water if the carrots stick to the pan.

3. When the carrots begin to soften, after about six minutes, add honey and butter. Cook for several more minutes until the carrots are tender, but not mushy.

Table Manners

In the Middle Ages, people valued polite table manners. They were taught to keep their hands and fingernails clean, not to wipe their mouths on tablecloths, and not to pick their teeth while at the table. It was considered impolite to slurp soup and to blow on food to cool it. People were supposed to eat slowly, take small bites, and offer others at the table the best bits of food.

▶ *Servants brought guests towels and water drawn from a well so they could wash their hands before each course.*

Medieval Gingerbread

Medieval "gingerbread" was a popular sweet. It did not always contain ginger, but it always had a spicy taste. It was often colored red, and each piece was decorated with leaves, cloves, and gold or silver foil. This recipe makes 20 to 30 small pieces of gingerbread.

Directions

1. Line the baking pans with two layers of waxed paper.

2. Warm the honey in a saucepan over low heat until it is very thin.

3. Stir in the spices. Add a few drops of red food coloring.

4. Gradually stir in the breadcrumbs, until the mixture is very thick but still shiny. If the mixture looks dry and crumbly, stir in a bit more honey.

5. Spread the mixture in the baking pans. With a spatula, smooth the top. Set in a cool place or in the refrigerator until cool to the touch, about 45 minutes.

6. Lift the cooled mixture out of the pan and cut it into shapes. Decorate the gingerbread with silver balls, candied fruit, or green candy leaves.

Gingerbread Ingredients

1 lb (.45 kg) pasteurized liquid honey
1 tsp (5 mL) ground ginger
2 tsp (10 mL) ground cinnamon
1/2 tsp (2 mL) ground white or black pepper
Red food coloring (optional)
1 lb (.45 kg) fine dried breadcrumbs, not seasoned
Silver balls, candied fruit, green candy leaves

Spiced Cider

The main drink at medieval feasts was wine served warm and flavored with spices. For your feast, you can warm store-bought apple cider over the stove or in a crockpot. Add cinnamon sticks, whole cloves, and peppercorns for a spicy flavor.

Feast Day!

On the day of your feast, decorate the room where you will hold your feast. Hang colorful pieces of cloth as well as the wall hangings and coats of arms you made. Cover the tables with white cloths and sprinkle with dried flowers and herbs. Put a name card at each place, and set the table with plates, spoons, napkins, and cups. Place a thick slice of bread on each plate.

Supplies

- Loose black tea or coffee grinds
- 9 inch by 12 inch (23 cm by 30 cm) baking pans
- Water
- Kettle or saucepan
- Sturdy white paper
- Fine black marker or felt-tip pen
- Gold, silver, and other colored markers
- Colored string, yarn or ribbon

Make Invitations

Invite teachers and students from other classes, family members, classroom volunteers, or the principal to your feast. Make invitations that look as if they were written on parchment.

Directions

1. Put tea leaves or coffee grinds into baking pans. Pour boiling water over the tea or coffee until the pans are about half full. Let the water cool to room temperature.

2. Tear sheets of paper in half lengthwise, then gently rip the edges so they look jagged.

3. Place the paper in the tea or coffee water for one hour.

From the students of classroom 10 Please join us at midday on the first of May to celebrate the arrival of spring.

4. When the paper is dry, use the lettering on page 21 to write your invitations.

5. Roll up the invitations and tie them with ribbon or yarn.

Serve the Meal

At a medieval feast, the food was usually served in three courses, or stages. The guests of honor, seated at the head table, were served each course first, with special care.

Servers in the Middle Ages had different duties. Pantlers served bread and made sure that important guests had loaves before them. Cupbearers brought goblets of wine to the head table. Other servers carved meat and carried platters. Decide who will do each job at your feast.

Entertain the Guests

Musicians, singers, dancers, jugglers, actors, and acrobats entertained guests at medieval feasts. Entertain your guests by singing songs, playing instruments, telling stories and jokes, or performing the puppet play you prepared on page 23.

Generosity and Giving

At the end of medieval feasts, hosts often gave important guests tapestries or jewels. Members of the household received clothes or coins. On many occasions, such as wedding feasts, small gifts of money, called alms, were given to poor people in the community. Women of the household also gave food left over from the feast to the poor and sick.

Hold a food drive on the day of your feast. Collect canned and dry foods and donate them to a local food bank or another community charity.

▶ *Dress up for your feast. Wear long shirts over your clothes. Add a belt, and look for items around your home that you can use as jewelry or head coverings. When medieval women prepared for a feast, they covered their long hair with elaborate headdresses, such as these tall hennin.*

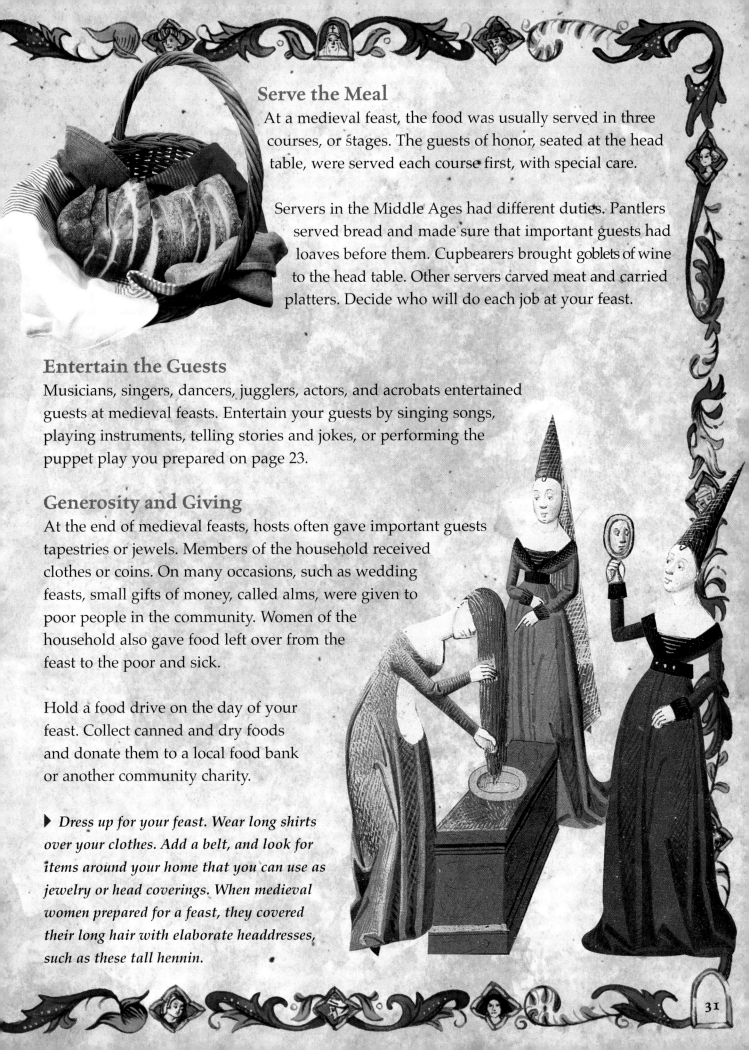

Glossary

ancestor A person from whom someone is descended

barter To trade goods without exchanging money

Bible The Christian holy book

ceramic Baked clay

document A piece of writing that contains important information

dye A substance used to color something such as fabric

embroider To make a design in cloth using a needle and thread

fortified Protected or strengthened against attacks

knight A medieval soldier who fought on horseback, mainly with a sword

Latin The language of the ancient Romans and the Roman Catholic Church

manor A noble's land

manuscript A text written by hand

mineral A substance obtained through mining

mortar A mixture of sand, lime, water, bricks, and stones

mythological Relating to myths, or traditional stories

noble A person born into a ruling class

Normandy A historical region in northwestern France

oak gall A swelling in the bark of an oak tree where insect eggs are laid. The gall contains acids used to make ink and tan leather

perishable Subject to decay or spoiling

possession Control over something

preserve To treat or store food to protect it from decay

quill The hollow shaft of a bird's feather

soot The fine black particles that result from burning wood, coal, and other types of fuel

tanned Animal skin or hide that has been treated to make leather

timber Wood used to create furniture, buildings, and other objects

Index

1 2 3 4 5 6 7 8 9 0   Printed in the U.S.A. 2 1 0 9 8 7 6 5